God's Little Instruction Book

Inspirational Wisdom on how to live a happy and fulfilled life.

HONOR

Honor Books, Inc. • P.O. Box 55388 • Tulsa, OK 74155

INTRODUCTION

God's Little Instruction Book is an inspirational collection of quotes and Scriptures that will motivate you to live a meaningful, productive and happy life. Some books have quotes, and some have Scriptures, but we wanted to combine both to provide not just man's insight, but to include the wisdom of the ages – God's Word.

This little book was designed and written to be fun to read, yet thought-provoking and one that will challenge you to reach for the best and fulfill your potential. We have filled it with quotes and sayings, familiar and unfamiliar, but we have also included a Scripture with each instruction that reveals what God's Word has to say about each topic.

Basic, practical and filled with the timeless wisdom of the Bible, this delightful book offers a road map to succeed in the daily journey of life. We here at Honor Books hope that you will learn to treasure *God's Little Instruction Book* as much as we have.

God's Little Instruction Book
ISBN 1-56292-044-8
Copyright © 1993 by Honor Books, Inc.
P.O. Box 55388
Tulsa, OK 74155

16th Printing
Over 1,175,000 in Print

A marriage may be made in heaven, but the maintenance must be done on earth.

Nevertheless let every one of you in particular so love his wife even as himself; and the wife see that she reverence her husband.
Ephesians 5:33

When God measures a man, He puts the tape around the heart instead of the head.

...the Lord seeth not as man seeth; for man looketh on the outward appearance, but the Lord looketh on the heart.
I Samuel 16:7b

The grass may look greener on the other side, but it still has to be mowed.

...And be content with such things as ye have...
Hebrews 13:5

Patience is the ability to keep your motor idling when you feel like stripping your gears.

He that is slow to anger is better than the mighty; and he that ruleth his spirit than he that taketh a city.
Proverbs 16:32

He who is waiting for something to turn up might start with his own shirt sleeves.

All hard work brings a profit,
but mere talk leads only to poverty.
Proverbs 14:23 (NIV)

Remember the banana – when it left the bunch, it got skinned.

Not forsaking the assembling of ourselves together, as the manner of some is; but exhorting one another: and so much the more, as ye see the day approaching.
Hebrews 10:25

It is better to be silent and be considered a fool than to speak and remove all doubt.

Yea also, when he that is a fool walketh by the way, his wisdom faileth him, and he saith to every one that he is a fool.
Ecclesiastes 10:3

Many a good man has failed because he had his wishbone where his backbone should have been.

Have not I commanded thee? Be strong and of a good courage; be not afraid, neither be thou dismayed: for the Lord thy God is with thee whithersoever thou goest.
Joshua 1:9

If at first you don't succeed, try reading the instructions.

*Take fast hold of instruction; let her not go:
keep her; for she is thy life.*
Proverbs 4:13

Your temper is like a fire. It gets very destructive when it gets out of control.

*He that hath no rule over his own spirit is like a city
that is broken down, and without walls.*
Proverbs 25:28

Decisions can take you out of God's will but never out of His reach.

If we are faithless, He will remain faithful,
for he cannot disown himself.
2 Timothy 2:13 (NIV)

Your companions are like the buttons on an elevator. They will either take you up or they will take you down.

He that walketh with wise men shall be wise: but a companion of fools shall be destroyed.
Proverbs 13:20

Patience is a quality you admire in the driver behind you and scorn in the one ahead.

The end of the matter is better than its beginning, and patience is better than pride. Do not be quickly provoked in your spirit, for anger resides in the lap of fools.
Ecclesiastes 7:8,9 (NIV)

There is a name for people who are not excited about their work – unemployed.

And whatsoever ye do, do it heartily,
as to the Lord, and not unto men;
Colossians 3:23

A person's true character is
revealed by what he does
when no one is watching.

*Obey them not only to win their favor when their eye is on you,
but like slaves of Christ, doing the will of God from your heart.*
Ephcsians 6:6 (NIV)

It's better to die with a good name than to live with a bad one.

A good name is better than precious ointment;
Ecclesiastes 7:1

"No" is one of the few
words that can never be
misunderstood.

But let your statement be "yes, yes" or "no, no"...
Matthew 5:37a (NASB)

Too many churchgoers are singing
"Standing on the Promises" when
all they are doing is sitting
on the premises.

*That ye be not slothful, but followers of them who through
faith and patience inherit the promises.*
Hebrews 6:12

Some people complain because
God put thorns on roses, while
others praise Him for putting
roses among thorns.

Finally, brethren, whatsoever things are true, whatsoever things are honest, whatsoever things are just, whatsoever things are pure, whatsoever things are lovely, whatsoever things are of good report; if there be any virtue, and if there be any praise, think on these things.
Philippians 4:8

The cure of crime is not in the electric chair, but in the high chair.

Train up a child in the way he should go:
and when he is old, he will not depart from it.
Proverbs 22:6

The bridge you burn now may be the one you later have to cross.

If it be possible, as much as lieth in you,
live peaceably with all men.
Romans 12:18

The measure of a man is not how great his faith is but how great his love is.

And now these three remain: faith, hope and love.
But the greatest of these is love.
1 Corinthians 13:13 (NIV)

Real friends are those who, when you've made a fool of yourself, don't feel you've done a permanent job.

Beareth all things, believeth all things, hopeth all things, endureth all things. Charity never faileth...
1 Corinthians 13:7,8

Be careful that your marriage doesn't become a duel instead of a duet.

Let us therefore follow after the things which make for peace, and things wherewith one may edify another.
Romans 14:19

The mighty oak was once a little nut that stood its ground.

A man shall not be established by wickedness: but the root of the righteous shall not be moved.
Proverbs 12:3

The secret of achievement is to not let what you're doing get to you before you get to it.

Commit thy works unto the Lord, and thy thoughts shall be established.
Proverbs 16:3

Most people wish to serve God – but only in an advisory capacity.

Humble yourselves therefore under the mighty hand of God,
that he may exalt you in due time:
1 Peter 5:6

Conscience is God's built-in warning system. Be very happy when it hurts you. Be very worried when it doesn't.

And herein do I exercise myself, to have always a conscience void of offence toward God, and toward men.
Acts 24:16

Most men forget God all day and ask Him to remember them at night.

*Evening, and morning, and at noon, will I pray, and
cry aloud: and he shall hear my voice.*
Psalm 55:17

If you don't stand for something you'll fall for anything!

...If you do not stand firm in your faith,
you will not stand at all.
Isaiah 7:9b (NIV)

The measure of a man's character is not what he gets from his ancestors, but what he leaves his descendants.

A good man leaveth an inheritance to his children's children: and the wealth of the sinner is laid up for the just.
Proverbs 13:22

Although the tongue weighs very little, few people are able to hold it.

Even so the tongue is a little member, and boasteth great things. Behold, how great a matter a little fire kindleth!
James 3:5

You should never let adversity get you down – except on your knees.

Is any one of you in trouble? He should pray...
James 5:13 a NIV

He who wants milk should not sit on a stool in the middle of the pasture expecting the cow to back up to him.

He becometh poor that dealeth with a slack hand: but the hand of the diligent maketh rich.
Proverbs 10:4

The best bridge between hope and despair is often a good night's sleep.

It is vain for you to rise up early, to sit up late, to eat the bread of sorrows: for so he giveth his beloved sleep.
Psalm 127:2

It is good to remember that the tea kettle, although up to its neck in hot water, continues to sing.

Rejoice evermore. In every thing give thanks: for this is the will of God in Christ Jesus concerning you.
I Thessalonians 5:16,18

It's good to be a Christian and know it, but it's better to be a Christian and show it!

By this shall all men know that ye are my disciples,
if ye have love one to another.
John 13:35

Sorrow looks back. Worry looks around. Faith looks up.

Fixing our eyes on Jesus, the author and perfecter of faith, who for the joy set before Him endured the cross, despising the shame, and has sat down at the right hand of the throne of God.
Hebrews 12:2 (NASB)

A man is never in worse company
than when he flies into a rage
and is beside himself.

He that is soon angry dealeth foolishly...
Proverbs 14:17a

Success in marriage is more than finding the right person. It's becoming the right person.

But thou, O man of God, flee these things; and follow after righteousness, godliness, faith, love, patience, meekness.
1 Timothy 6:11

Failure in people is caused more by lack of determination than lack in talent.

And let us not be weary in well doing:
for in due season we shall reap, if we faint not.
Galatians 6:9

A man is rich according to what he *is*, not according to what he *has*.

There is that maketh himself rich, yet hath nothing: there is that maketh himself poor, yet hath great riches.
Proverbs 13:7

Life can only be understood by looking backward, but it must be lived by looking forward.

And Jesus said unto him, "No man, having put his hand to the plough, and looking back, is fit for the kingdom of God."
Luke 9:62

Success comes in cans;
failure comes in can'ts.

I can do all things through Christ which strengtheneth me.
Philippians 4:13

Sometimes we are so busy adding up our troubles that we forget to count our blessings.

I will remember the works of the Lord: surely I will remember thy wonders of old. I will meditate also of all thy work, and talk of thy doings.
Psalm 77:11, 12

Falling down doesn't make you a failure, but staying down does.

For a just man falleth seven times, and riseth up again...
Proverbs 24:16a

If a task is once begun,
Never leave it 'till it's done.
Be the labor great or small,
Do it well or not at all.

*I have glorified thee on the earth: I have finished
the work which thou gavest me to do.*
John 17:4

Time is more valuable than money because time is irreplaceable.

Redeeming the time, because the days are evil.
Ephesians 5:16

The best way to forget your own problems is to help someone solve his.

Look not every man on his own things, but every man also on the things of others.
Philippians 2:4

God can heal a broken heart, but he has to have all the pieces.

My son, give me thine heart...
Proverbs 23:26a

Authority makes some people grow – and others just swell.

But he that is greatest among you shall be your servant.
And whosoever shall exalt himself shall be abased;
and he that shall humble himself shall be exalted.
Matthew 23:11,12

Be more concerned with what God thinks about you than what people think about you.

Then Peter and the other apostles answered and said,
"We ought to obey God rather than men."
Acts 5:29

The trouble with the guy who talks too fast is that he often says something he hasn't thought of yet.

Be not rash with thy mouth, and let not thine heart be hasty to utter any thing before God: for God is in heaven, and thou upon earth: therefore let thy words be few.
Ecclesiastes 5:2

The best way to get the last word is to apologize.

If you have been trapped by what you said, ensnared by the words of your mouth, then do this, my son, to free yourself, since you have fallen into your neighbor's hands: Go and humble yourself; press your plea with your neighbor!
Proverbs 6:2,3 (NIV)

The train of failure usually runs on the track of laziness.

By much slothfulness the building decayeth; and through idleness of the hands the house droppeth through.
Ecclesiastes 10:18

When confronted with a Goliath-sized problem, which way do you respond: "He's too big to hit" or, like David, "He's too big to miss"?

...The LORD that delivered me out of the paw of the lion, and out of the paw of the bear, he will deliver me out of the hand of this Philistine.
I Samuel 17:37

Forget yourself for others and others will not forget you!

Therefore all things whatsoever ye would that men should do to you, do ye even so to them: for this is the law and the prophets.
Matthew 7:12

The secret of success is to start from scratch and keep on scratching.

And the seed in the good soil, these are the ones who have heard the word in an honest and good heart, and hold it fast, and bear fruit with perseverance.
Luke 8:15 NASB

The secret of contentment is the realization that life is a gift not a right.

But godliness with contentment is great gain. For we brought nothing into this world, and it is certain we can carry nothing out.
1 Timothy 6:6,7

No one ever said on their deathbed: I wish I would have spent more time at work!

Yea, I hated all my labour which I had taken under the sun: because I should leave it unto the man that shall be after me. Ecclesiastes 2:18

And whatsoever ye do, do it heartily, as to the Lord, and not unto men. Colossians 3:23

True faith and courage are like a kite – an opposing wind raises it higher.

But they that wait upon the LORD shall renew their strength; they shall mount up with wings as eagles; they shall run, and not be weary; and they shall walk, and not faint.
Isaiah 40:31

In order to receive the direction
from God you must be able to
receive the correction from God.

*...My son, despise not thou the chastening of the Lord, nor faint when
thou art rebuked of him: For whom the Lord loveth he chasteneth,
and scourgeth every son whom he receiveth.*
Hebrews 12:5b,6

Those who bring sunshine to the lives of others cannot keep it from themselves.

Be not deceived; God is not mocked:
for whatsoever a man soweth, that shall he also reap.
Galatians 6:7

No man ever really finds out what he believes in until he begins to instruct his children.

And, ye fathers, provoke not your children to wrath: but bring them up in the nurture and admonition of the Lord.
Ephesians 6:4

Don't mistake activity for achievement. Busyness does not equal productiveness.

But Martha was cumbered about much serving, and came to him, and said, Lord, dost thou not care that my sister hath left me to serve alone? bid her therefore that she help me. And Jesus answered and said unto her, "Martha, Martha, thou art careful and troubled about many things: But one thing is needful: and Mary hath chosen that good part, which shall not be taken away from her."
Luke 10:40-42

It's the little things in life that determine the big things.

...Thou hast been faithful over a few things, I will make thee ruler over many things: enter thou into the joy of thy lord.
Matthew 25:21b

The doors of opportunity are marked "Push" and "Pull."

The soul of the sluggard desireth, and hath nothing:
but the soul of the diligent shall be made fat.
Proverbs 13:4

You cannot win
if you do not begin.

Now therefore perform the doing of it; that as there was a
readiness to will, so there may be a performance also
out of that which ye have.
2 Corinthians 8:11

The best way to be successful is to follow the advice you give others.

He who ignores discipline despises himself,
but whoever heeds correction gains understanding.
Proverbs 15:32 (NIV)

Contentment isn't getting what we want but being satisfied with what we have.

Not that I speak in respect of want: for I have learned,
in whatsoever state I am, therewith to be content.
Philippians 4:11

Too many people quit looking for work when they find a job.

He also that is slothful in his work
is brother to him that is a great waster.
Proverbs 18:9

You can't take your money with you, but you can send it on ahead.

Lay not up for yourselves treasures upon earth, where moth and rust doth corrupt, and where thieves break through and steal: But lay up for yourselves treasures in heaven, where neither moth nor rust doth corrupt, and where thieves do not break through nor steal.

Matthew 6:19,20

Ability will enable a man to go to the top, but it takes character to keep him there.

The righteousness of the blameless makes a straight way for them,
but the wicked are brought down by their own wickedness.
Proverbs 11:5 (NIV)

Your words are
windows to your heart.

...For out of the abundance of the heart the mouth speaketh.
Matthew 12:34b

A shut mouth
gathers no foot.

He that keepeth his mouth keepeth his life: but he that openeth wide his lips shall have destruction.
Proverbs 13:3

The only fool bigger than the person who knows it all is the person who argues with him.

He that reproveth a scorner getteth to himself shame: and he that rebuketh a wicked man getteth himself a blot.
Proverbs 9:7

A drowning man does not complain about the size of a life preserver.

Do all things without murmurings and disputings.
Philippians 2:14

Blessed is he who, having nothing to say, refrains from giving wordy evidence of the fact.

The tongue of the wise useth knowledge aright:
but the mouth of fools poureth out foolishness.
Proverbs 15:2

Luck: a loser's excuse for a winner's position.

The soul of the sluggard desireth, and hath nothing:
but the soul of the diligent shall be made fat.
Proverbs 13:4

Do the thing you fear and the death of fear is certain.

Be strong and of a good courage, fear not, nor be afraid of them:
for the LORD thy God, he it is that doth go with thee;
he will not fail thee, nor forsake thee.
Deuteronomy 31:6

God plus one
is always a majority!

...If God be for us, who can be against us?
Romans 8:31b

Whoever gossips to you will be a gossip of you.

A talebearer revealeth secrets: but he that is of a faithful spirit concealeth the matter.
Proverbs 11:13

Jesus is a friend who knows all your faults and still loves you anyway.

But God commendeth his love toward us, in that, while we were yet sinners, Christ died for us.
Romans 5:8

Every person should have a special cemetery lot in which to bury the faults of friends and loved ones.

And be ye kind one to another, tenderhearted, forgiving one another, even as God for Christ's sake hath forgiven you.
Ephesians 4:32

Ignorance is always swift to speak.

...Let every man be swift to hear, slow to speak, slow to wrath.
James 1:19b

Learn from other's mistakes rather than making them all yourself.

The way of a fool is right in his own eyes:
but he that hearkeneth unto counsel is wise.
Proverbs 12:15

Pick your friends
but not to pieces.

A man that beareth false witness against his neighbour
is a maul, and a sword, and a sharp arrow.
Proverbs 25:18

He who throws dirt
loses ground.

Wherefore putting away lying, speak every man truth with his neighbour: for we are members one of another.
Ephesians 4:25

You don't have to lie awake nights to succeed – just stay awake days.

I must work the works of him that sent me, while it is day: the night cometh, when no man can work.
John 9:4

The first step to wisdom is silence; the second is listening.

A wise man will hear, and will increase learning; and a man of understanding shall attain unto wise counsels.
Proverbs 1:5

The greatest possession you have is the 24 hours directly in front of you.

...For there is a time there for every purpose and for every work.
Ecclesiastes 3:17b

The most valuable gift you can give another is a good example.

For I have given you an example,
that ye should do as I have done to you.
John 13:15

Don't be afraid of pressure.
Remember that pressure is
what turns a lump of coal
into a diamond.

Knowing this, that the trying of your faith worketh patience. But let patience have her perfect work, that ye may be perfect and entire, wanting nothing.
James 1:3,4

A minute of thought is worth more than an hour of talk.

Set a watch, O Lord, before my mouth; keep the door of my lips.
Psalms 141:3

You can win
more friends with your ears
than with your mouth.

...Let every man be swift to hear, slow to speak, slow to wrath.
James 1:19b

It's not the outlook but the uplook that counts.

Looking unto Jesus the author and finisher of our faith...
Hebrews 12:2a

Put others before yourself, and you can become a leader among men.

But it shall not be so among you: but whosoever will be great among you, let him be your minister; And whosoever will be chief among you, let him be your servant.
Matthew 20:26,27

Feed your faith and your doubts will starve to death.

But we are not of those who shrink back to destruction,
but of those who have faith to the preserving of the soul.
Hebrews 10:39 (NASB)

Never pass up a chance to keep your mouth shut.

Even a fool, when he holdeth his peace, is counted wise:
and he that shutteth his lips is esteemed a man of understanding.
Proverbs 17:28

It isn't hard to make a mountain out of a molehill. Just add a little dirt.

Starting a quarrel is like breaching a dam;
so drop the matter before a dispute breaks out.
Proverbs 17:14 (NIV)

What counts is not the number of hours you put in, but how much you put in the hours.

Whatsoever thy hand findeth to do, do it with thy might...
Ecclesiastes 9:10a

Reputation is made in a moment: character is built in a lifetime.

My righteousness I hold fast, and will not let it go:
my heart shall not reproach me so long as I live.
Job 27:6

If you feel "dog tired" at night, maybe it's because you "growled" all day!

If it be possible, as much as lieth in you, live peaceably with all men.
Romans 12:18

If you don't want the fruits of sin, stay out of the devil's orchard.

Abstain from all appearance of evil.
I1 Thessalonians 5:22

Our children are like mirrors – they reflect our attitudes in life.

*The just man walketh in his integrity:
his children are blessed after him.*
Proverbs 20:7

The art of being a good guest is knowing when to leave.

Withdraw thy foot from thy neighbour's house;
lest he be weary of thee, and so hate thee.
Proverbs 25:17

He who cannot forgive
breaks the bridge over which
he himself must pass.

For if ye forgive men their trespasses,
your heavenly Father will also forgive you.
Matthew 6:14

Jesus is a friend who walks in when the world has walked out.

These things I have spoken unto you, that in me ye might have peace.
In the world ye shall have tribulation: but be of good cheer;
I have overcome the world.
John 16:33

Those who deserve love the least need it the most.

*But I say unto you, Love your enemies, bless them that curse you,
do good to them that hate you, and pray for them which
despitefully use you, and persecute you.*
Matthew 5:44

Faith is daring the soul to go beyond what the eyes can see.

For we walk by faith, not by sight.
2 Corinthians 5:7

The right angle to approach a difficult problem is the "try-angle."

For with God nothing shall be impossible.
Luke 1:37

The fellow who does things that count doesn't usually stop to count them.

Brothers, I do not consider myself yet to have taken hold of it.
But one thing I do: Forgetting what is behind and straining
toward what is ahead, ...
Philippians 3:13

A critical spirit is like poison ivy – it only takes a little contact to spread its poison.

But avoid wordly and empty chatter, for it will lead to further ungodliness, and their talk will spread like gangrene...
2 Timothy 2:16, 17a (NASB)

Laziness and poverty
are cousins.

Yet a little sleep, a little slumber, a little folding of the hands to sleep:
So shall thy poverty come as one that travelleth;
and thy want as an armed man.
Proverbs 24: 33,34

Language is the expression of thought. Every time you speak, your mind is on parade.

A good man out of the good treasure of his heart bringeth forth
that which is good; and an evil man out of the evil treasure
of his heart bringeth forth that which is evil:
for of the abundance of the heart his mouth speaketh.
Luke 6:45

Take care of your character and your reputation will take care of itself.

For bodily exercise profiteth little: but godliness is profitable unto all things, having promise of the life that now is, and of that which is to come. 1 Timothy 4:8

A good man leaveth an inheritance to his children's children: and the wealth of the sinner is laid up for the just. Proverbs 13:22

The hardest secret
for a man to keep is
his opinion of himself.

For I say, through the grace given unto me, to every man that is among you, not to think of himself more highly than he ought to think; but to think soberly, according as God hath dealt to every man the measure of faith.
Romans 12:3

He who buries his talent is making a grave mistake.

Neglect not the gift that is in thee...
1 Timothy 4:14a

If a care is too small to be turned into a prayer, it is too small to be made into a burden.

Casting all your care upon him; for he careth for you.
1 Peter 5:7

Even a woodpecker owes his success to the fact that he uses his head.

But you, keep your head in all situations...
2 Timothy 4:5

The poorest of all men is not the man without a cent but the man without a dream.

Where there is no vision, the people perish...
Proverbs 29:18a

You can accomplish more in one hour with God than one lifetime without Him.

...With God all things are possible.
Matthew 19:26b

The only preparation for tomorrow is the right use of today.

Take therefore no thought for the morrow: for the morrow shall take thought for the things of itself. Sufficient unto the day is the evil thereof.
Matthew 6:34

When things go wrong, don't go wrong with them.

*Enter not into the path of the wicked, and go
not in the way of evil men.*
Proverbs 4:14

Two things are hard on the heart – running up stairs and running down people.

Let no corrupt communication proceed out of your mouth, but that which is good to the use of edifying, that it may minister grace unto the hearers.
Ephesians 4:29

The best way to get even is to forget.

But love ye your enemies, and do good, and lend, hoping for nothing again; and your reward shall be great, and ye shall be the children of the Highest: for he is kind unto the unthankful and to the evil.
Luke 6:35

People don't care how much you know until they know how much you care.

Let nothing be done through strife or vainglory; but in lowliness of mind let each esteem other better than themselves.
Philippians 2:3

Humor is to life
what shock absorbers are
to automobiles.

A merry heart doeth good like a medicine:
but a broken spirit drieth the bones.
Proverbs 17:22

A man wrapped up in himself makes a very small package.

*A fool finds no pleasure in understanding but
delights in airing his own opinions.*
Proverbs 18:2 (NIV)

It isn't your position that makes you happy or unhappy, it's your disposition.

But godliness with contentment is great gain. For we brought nothing into this world, and it is certain we can carry nothing out.
I Timothy 6:6, 7

It takes more to plow a field than merely turning it over in your mind.

...work with your hands, just as we commanded you, so that you may behave properly toward outsiders and not be in any need.
1 Thessalonians 4:11, 12 (NASB)

Men are like fish.
Neither would get into trouble
if they kept their mouths shut.

*Whoso keepeth his mouth and his tongue
keepeth his soul from troubles.*
Proverbs 21:23

The heart of a man cannot be determined by the size of his pocketbook.

For what shall it profit a man, if he shall gain the whole world, and lose his own soul? Or what shall a man give in exchange for his soul?
Mark 8:36,37

Kindness is the oil that takes the friction out of life.

But the fruit of the Spirit is ...kindness
Galatians 5:22 (NIV)

You can easily determine the caliber of a person by the amount of opposition it takes to discourage him.

If thou faint in the day of adversity, thy strength is small.
Proverbs 24:10

People know what you are by what they see, not by what they hear.

Let your light so shine before men, that they may see your good works, and glorify your Father which is in heaven.
Matthew 5:16

People who try to whittle you down are only trying to reduce you to their size.

Blessed are ye, when men shall hate you, and when they shall separate you from their company, and shall reproach you, and cast out your name as evil, for the Son of man's sake. Rejoice ye in that day, and leap for joy: for, behold, your reward is great in heaven...
Luke 6:22,23a

Quite often when a man thinks his mind is getting broader, it's only his conscience stretching.

Unto the pure all things are pure: but unto them that are defiled and unbelieving is nothing pure; but even their mind and conscience is defiled.
Titus 1:15

Temper is what gets most of us into trouble. Pride is what keeps us there.

Pride goeth before destruction, and an haughty spirit before a fall.
Better it is to be of an humble spirit with the lowly,
than to divide the spoil with the proud.
Proverbs 16:18,19

We make a living by what we get – we make a life by what we give.

I have shewed you all things, how that so labouring ye ought to support the weak, and to remember the words of the Lord Jesus, how he said, It is more blessed to give than to receive.

Acts 20:35

Our days are identical suitcases –
all the same size – but some
people can pack more into
them than others.

Be very careful, then, how you live — not as unwise but as wise,
making the most of every opportunity....
Ephesians 5:15,16 (NIV)

Living would be easier if men showed as much patience at home as they do when they're fishing.

You husbands likewise, live with your wives in an understanding way...
1 Peter 3:7b (NASB)

Some people succeed because
they are destined to, but most
people succeed because they
are determined to.

...and having done all, to stand. Stand therefore...
Ephesians 6:13, 14a

A man is rich according to what he is, not according to what he has.

There is that maketh himself rich, yet hath nothing: there is that maketh himself poor, yet hath great riches.
Proverbs 13:7

The difference between ordinary and extraordinary is that little extra.

Whatsoever thy hand findeth to do, do it with thy might; for there is no work, nor device, nor knowledge, nor wisdom, in the grave, whither thou goest.
Ecclesiastes 9:10

Swallowing angry words is much better than having to eat them.

A fool uttereth all his mind: but a wise man keepeth it in till afterwards.
Proverbs 29:11

To forgive is to set a prisoner free and discover the prisoner was YOU.

For if ye forgive men their trespasses, your heavenly Father will also forgive you: But if ye forgive not men their trespasses, neither will your Father forgive your trespasses.
Matthew 6:14,15

The company you keep will determine the trouble you meet.

Make no friendship with an angry man; and with a furious man thou shalt not go: Lest thou learn his ways, and get a snare to thy soul.
Proverbs 22:24,25

Too many parents are not on spanking terms with their children.

He who spares his rod hates his son.
But he who loves him disciplines him diligently.
Proverbs 13:24 (NASB)

Man cannot discover new oceans unless he has the courage to lose sight of the shore.

And Peter answered him and said, Lord, if it be thou, bid me come unto thee on the water. And he said, "Come." And when Peter was come down out of the ship, he walked on the water, to go to Jesus.
Matthew 14:28,29

The heart is the happiest when it beats for others.

Greater love hath no man than this, that a man lay down his life for his friends.
John 15:13

One thing you can learn by
watching the clock is that it
passes time by keeping
its hands busy.

*He also that is slothful in his work is brother
to him that is a great waster.*
Proverbs 18:9

Now there's even a "dial-a-prayer" for atheists. You call a number and nobody answers.

The fool hath said in his heart, There is no God...
Psalm 14:1a

He who thinks by the inch and talks by the yard deserves to be kicked by the foot.

A fool's lips bring him strife, and his mouth invites a beating.
Proverbs 18:6 (NIV)

The best inheritance a father can leave his children is a good example.

As ye know how we exhorted and comforted and charged every one of you, as a father doth his children.
1 Thessalonians 2:11

God intervenes in the affairs of men by invitation only.

*Behold, I stand at the door, and knock: if any man hear my voice,
and open the door, I will come in to him, and will
sup with him, and he with me.*
Revelation 3:20